Little Pebble

Our Fa...

# Sisters
## Are Part of a Family

by Lucia Raatma

CAPSTONE PRESS
a capstone imprint

Little Pebble is published by Capstone Press,
1710 Roe Crest Drive, North Mankato, Minnesota 56003
www.mycapstone.com

**Library of Congress Cataloging-in-Publication Data is available
on the Library of Congress website**

ISBN: 978-1-5157-7460-0 (library binding)
ISBN: 978-1-5157-7470-9 (paperback)
written by Lucia Raatma

**Editorial Credits**
Christianne Jones, editor; Juliette Peters, designer;
Wanda Winch, media researcher; Laura Manthe, production specialist

**Photo Credits**
Capstone Studio: Karon Dubke, 11, 15, 17, 21, Juliette Peters, 9; Shutterstock: Angelina
Babii, paper texture, Golden Pixels LLC, 7, Mila Supinskaya Glashchenko, 5, MNStudio, 19,
Pressmaster, 13, Ronnachai Palas, cover, Samuel Borges Photography, 1, Teguh Mujiono,
tree design

Printed in the United States        5329

# Table of Contents

# Sisters

Sisters are family. They may have brothers. They may also have sisters.

Mae is a big sister.
She has a sister and
a brother.

Grace and Eli are twins.
They were born on the
same day.

Maria has a brother.

Her brother is a baby.

# What Sisters Do

Sky likes to ride her bike.

She rides with her brothers.

Ana's sister likes to read.

She reads to Ana.

Devon's sister likes to play games. Devon plays with her.

Violet likes to play soccer.

So does her sister.

Sisters play.

They giggle.

They love.

# Glossary

**brother**—a boy who has the same parents as another person

**giggle**—to laugh in a silly way

**sister**—a girl who has the same parents as another person

**twin**—one of two children born at the same time to the same parents

# Read More

Robie H. *Who's in My Family? All About Our Families.* Somerville, MA: Candlewick, 2012.

Hunter, Nick. *Finding Out About Your Family History.* Mankato, MN: Heinemann-Raintree, 2015.

Lewis, Clare. *Familes Around the World.* Mankato, MN: Heinemann-Raintree, 2015.

# Internet Sites

FactHound offers a safe, fun way to find Internet sites related to this book. All of the sites on FactHound have been researched by our staff.

Here's all you do:
Visit *www.facthound.com*
Type in this code: 9781515774600

Super-cool stuff! Check out projects, games and lots more at **www.capstonekids.com**

# Index